A Very Mice
Joke Book

A Very Mice
Joke Book

illustrated
by
Lynn Mousinger
Munsinger

BY KAREN JO GOUNAUD

HOUGHTON MIFFLIN COMPANY

Boston 1981

Dedicated to all our loving
friends in Mouseachusetts

Library of Congress Cataloging in Publication Data

Gounaud, Karen Jo.
   A very mice joke book.
     SUMMARY: A collection of jokes about the behavior
of "Fay Mouse" and lesser known mice.
     1. Riddles, Juvenile. 2. Wit and humor,
Juvenile. 3. Mice—Anecdotes, facetiae, satire,
etc. [1. Riddles. 2. Mice—Anecdotes, facetiae,
satire, etc.] I. Title.
PN6371.G68   818' .5402   80-25413
ISBN 0-395-30445-8 (lib. bdg.)
ISBN 0-395-30442-3 (pbk.)

Printed in the United States of America.

Y 10 9 8 7 6 5 4 3 2 1

A Very Mice Foreword

A Very Mice Joke Book really has *four* authors. Son Kevin, daughter Kristi, and husband Roger all contributed to the storehouse of Gounaud mouse jokes. In fact, the entire project was begun by eight-year-old Kevin, who volunteered the very first mouse joke at dinner one night. Because we had agreed to replace serious, current-events talk with light conversation, he started us off with: "What do you get when a mouse crawls into your lawn mower?" "Shredded *squeak*." A family of pun lovers, we eagerly followed his lead and began keeping a notebook of our collective ideas.

Mouse-mania dominated many supper times thereafter, spread to other world-weary friends, and infiltrated even my husband's office. But our greatest source of outside inspiration was the "very mice" congregation of the West Chelmsford United Methodist Church . . . in *Mouse*achusetts, naturally.

May *A Very Mice Joke Book* bring renewed good humor into your life as it has into ours, because "a merry heart doeth good like a medicine" (Proverbs 17:29); or, as one contemporary sage put it, "He who laughs, *lasts!*"

Karen Jo Gounaud

Who is the most agreeable mouse?

U. Nanny *Mouse*

Which mouse learned to pick locks?

Mick Key *Mouse*

Which mouse is in charge of the mail?

The Post*mouse*ter General

Name a historic mouse dictator.

*Mouse*olini

What does Sherlock Mouse do for a living?

He solves *mouse*teries

What was Teddy Roosevelt Mouse's
favorite saying?

"Squeak softly and carry a big stick"

Which mice travel in space?

*Mouse*tronauts

Who is the largest mouse in the world?

E. Norm *Mouse*

Who is the prettiest mouse in the country?

Mouse America

Which mouse introduces the acts in a talent show?

The *Mouse*ter of Ceremonies

Who is the best-known mouse author?

A. Nonny *Mouse*

Who told Southern mouse stories over and over?

Uncle Re*mouse*

What does a 500-pound mouse say?

———

"Here kitty, kitty, kitty..."

Name a very mice drama that won a
Pulitzer Prize.

———

The *Mice* Man Cometh

Which mouse wrote the Declaration of
Independence?

Tom *Mouse* Jefferson

Name two mice genders.

*Mouse*culine and feminine

Who led the mice out of captivity?

*Mouse*s

Where did he lead them?

To the Pro*mouse*d Land

Which mouse works for Lipton?

My tea *Mouse*

What do you call the conductor of an
all-mouse orchestra?

*Mice*tro

What kind of horses do mice cowboys ride?

*Mouse*tangs

Who is the best-known mouse of all?

———————

Fay *Mouse*

Who delivers memos in mice corporations?

*Mouse*engers

Isn't the president of Miceland important, too?

Not very. No one ever remembers who
was the *Mice* president

How can you tell when a mouse is too cold?

When he becomes a *mice*cicle

What do mice watch when they want a
good scare?

*Mouse*ter movies

What four-letter word do mice use when
they get angry?

———

Rats!

What do you give a mouse with a sore back?

A *Mouse*sage

When do mice cry?

When they are *mouse*erable

Where was the land of ancient Asian mice?

In *Mouse*opotamia

Where are the world's coldest mice?

*Mice*land

What is the capital of Miceland?

---

*Mouse*cow

Where do mice go to get their prescriptions
filled?

———

A phar*mouse*y

Where did mice hang out in the 1920s?

———

In *squeak*easies

Where do mice go to rest in peace?

To a *Mouse*oleum

Where did the mice land when they first got to America?

Ply*mouse* Rock

Where do mice like to beat their feet?

On the *Mouse*issippi mud

What games do mice play at parties?

*Mouse*ical chairs

What holiday honors brave mice?

Ar*mouse*tice Day

For what holiday do young mice hang up
their stockings?

Chris *Mouse* Day

Where do mice wear costumes?

To a *mouse*querade

What do mice wear to school on gym days?

Squeakers

Why do girl mice always beat boy mice
in a race?

Because *mice* guys always finish last

Name a mice police show.

The *Squeaks* of San Francisco

Why do mice go to college?

To get a *Mouse*ter's degree

What well-known mouse book was made into
a popular TV show?

Little *Mouse* on the Prairie

How do mice govern themselves?

With a Senate and a *Mouse* of Representatives

What do mice use to play their favorite songs?

A *Mouse* organ

What does a mice artist call his greatest work?

A *mouse*terpiece

Why do mice lift weights?

To get big *mouse*ls

What happens when they overdo it?

They get *mouse*l bound

What sport do mice athletes excell in?

Mice hockey

How do mice get to work in the city?

They ride on the *mouse* transit system

What do mice mothers read in their spare time?

Good *Mouse*keeping

How do mice drivers find their way on
long trips?

With *rode*nt maps

What do mice learn in first-aid class?

Mouse-to-*mouse* resuscitation

Why do cats need lots of erasers?

Because they're always making *mouse*takes

Why did the cat get a raise?

He did a *Mice* job

35

What pudding dessert do cats love best?

Chocolate *mouse*

What do hot cats drink in the summer time?

Mice tea

What do cats put in their drinks to keep them cold?

Mice cubes

What do cats use to decorate their birthday cakes?

*Mice*ing

What do cats put on their hot dogs?

*Mouse*tard

What do cats use for crispy salads?

*Mice*berg lettuce

What do cats order when they go to
a fancy restaurant?

Porter*mouse* steaks

What do cats put in their hot chocolate?

*Mouse*mallows

What do cats serve at birthday parties?

Cake and *mice* cream

What does a middle-class cat have
inside his refrigerator?

An automatic *mice* maker

How did the mouse lose part of his tail?

Cat Nip!

Why was the cat arrested?

He was caught committing a *mouse*demeanor

What happens when ten mice meet a
hundred cats?

*Mouse*acre

How does a cat use a telephone?

He talks into the *mouse*piece

Why do mice prefer peace and quiet?

Because no *mews* is good *mews*

How does a mouse outsmart a cat?

By *mouse*merizing him

What do cats kiss under at Christmastime?

*Mouse*ltoe

What do you throw at newlywed cats?

White *mice*

What kind of mice bite cats?

*Mouse*quitos

What is a cat's favorite subject in school?

Chem*mouse*try

What should you give mice with bad breath?

*Mouse*wash

How does a mouse disguise himself?

With a *mouse*tache

What do you call widespread panic in mice?

Mouse hysteria

What goes "Snap, Crackle, and Squeak"?

Mice Krispies

Why do mice like to beat the clock?

Because the clock _struck_ one!

Why did the mouse get a job at the dairy?

He wanted to become a _Big Cheese_

How do you greet an Israeli mouse?

*Mouse*eltov!

Which mice are the best speakers?

Toast*mouse*ters

Name a literary classic about French mice.

———————

Les *Mouse*erables